Once upon a time three billy goats lived in a field which had no grass.
Over the bridge they could see a field of long, green grass, but under the bridge lived a big, bad troll.
One day the little goat looked at the field of long, green grass.
He felt very hungry.

'I want to eat the grass,' said the little goat.

The little goat ran on to the bridge.

The troll jumped up.
'I am a troll, a big, big troll.
I want to eat you.'

'No, no, no,'
said the little goat.
'You can eat the big goat.'

The big goat ran on to the bridge.

The troll jumped up.
'I am a troll, a big, big troll.
I want to eat you.'

'No, no,' said the big goat.
'You can eat the big, big goat.'

The big, big goat ran on to the bridge.

The troll jumped up.
'I am a troll, a big, big troll.
I want to eat you.'

'No, you will not,'
said the big, big goat.
'In you go.'

'Now we can eat the grass,' said the goats.